Mrs Barn...

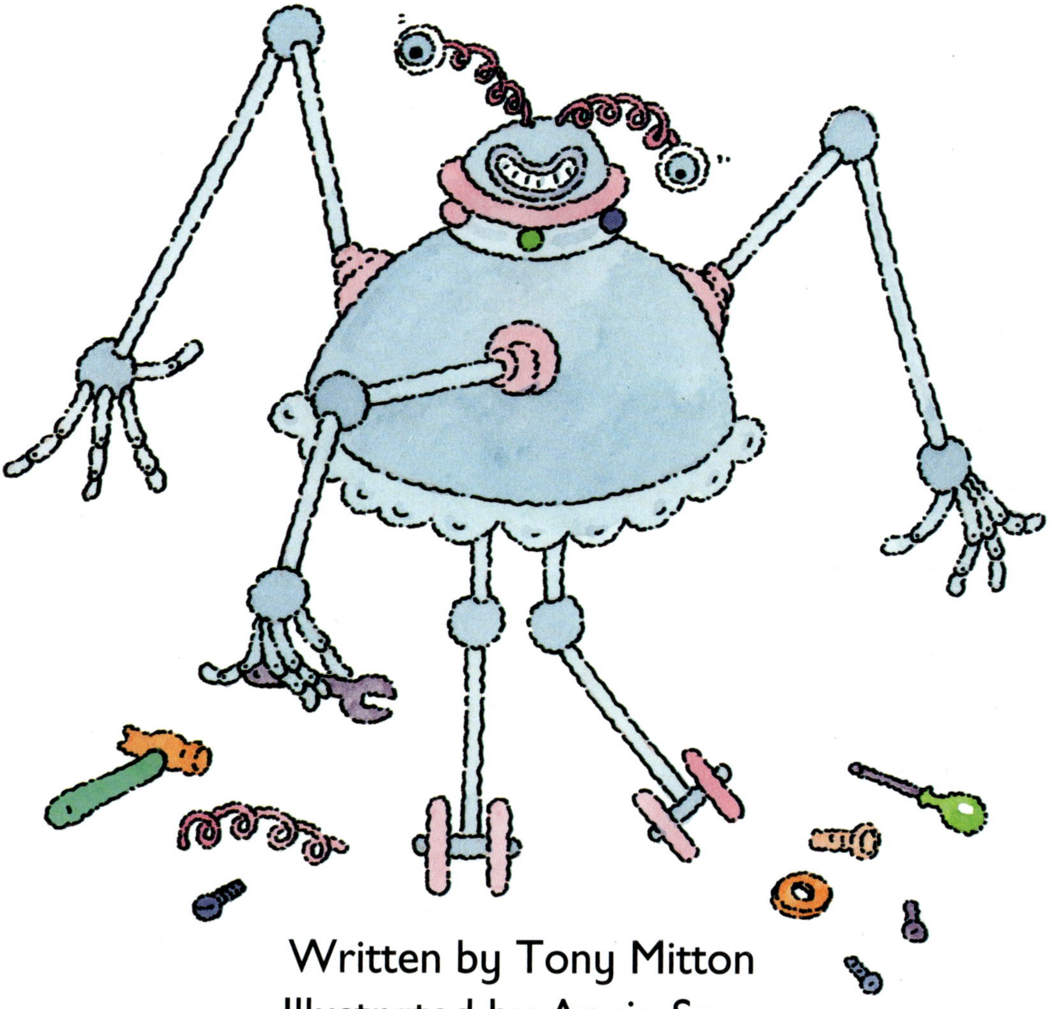

Written by Tony Mitton
Illustrated by Angie Sage

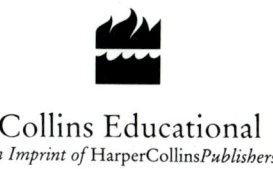

Collins Educational
An Imprint of HarperCollinsPublishers

Mrs Barmy made an amazing machine.

On the first day it woke
her up with a cup of tea.

On the second day it brushed her hair and cleaned her teeth.

On the third day it got her out of bed and dressed her.

But... on the fourth day it woke her up with a cup of toothpaste.

Then it brushed her feet with a hairbrush.

Then it put her pants on her head and her socks on her hands.

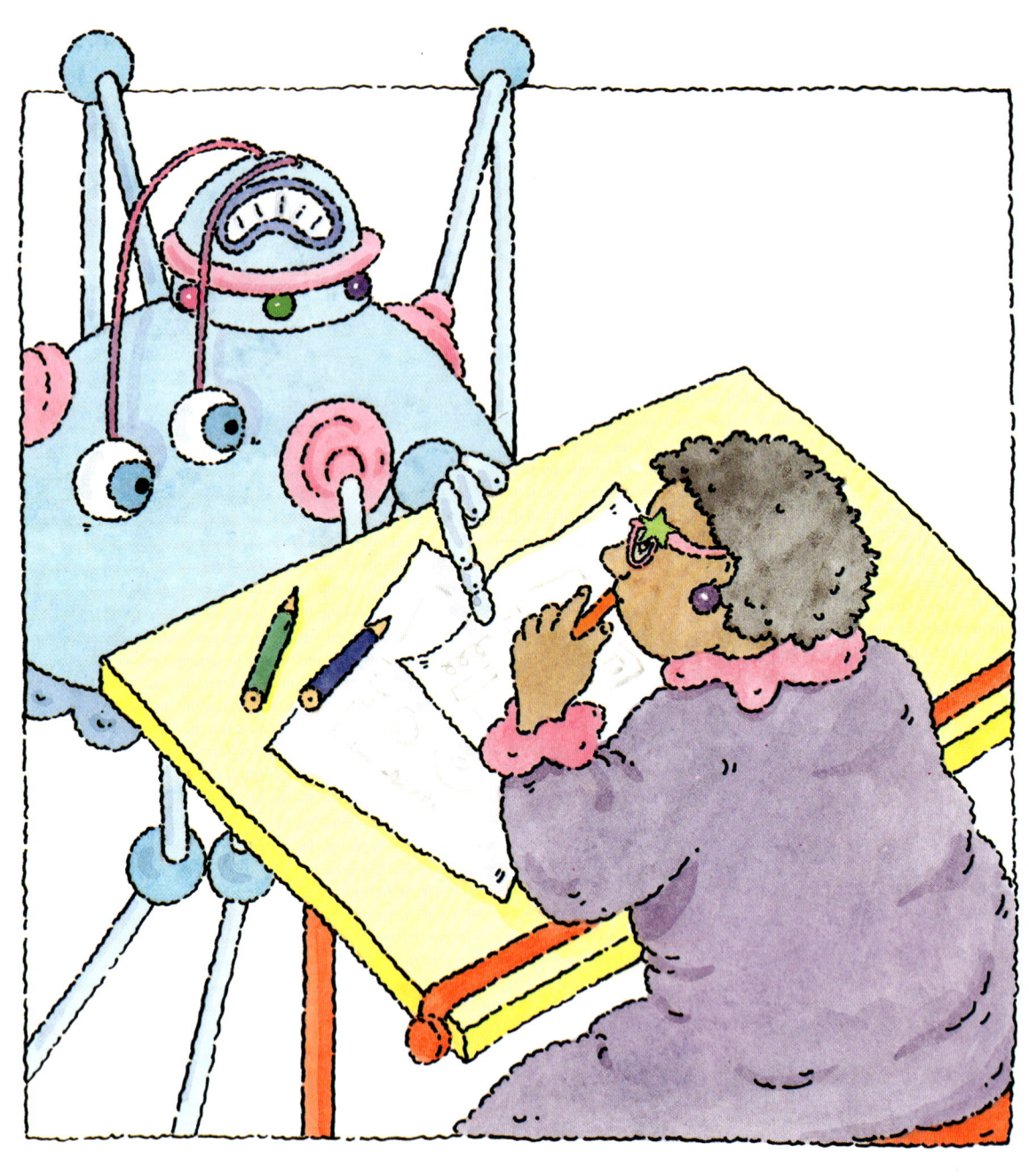

"Back to work,"
said Mrs Barmy crossly.